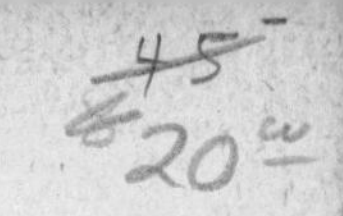

D1095051

FRANCO'S BLACK SPAIN

FRANCO'S BLACK SPAIN

DRAWINGS BY

LUIS QUINTANILLA

WITH A COMMENTARY BY RICHARD WATTS, JR.

REYNAL & HITCHCOCK, NEW YORK

PRINTED IN THE U.S.A BY THE GALLERY PRESS 287

INTRODUCTION

Most Americans have a guilty conscience about Spain—and this book will not make them feel any less guilty. Only too late have they come to realize what a few had long tried to tell them: that what was going on in that sad, brave country in the days before the official outbreak of the Second World War was neither a meaningless fratricidal strife nor a crusade in defense of Christian civilization, but the tragic prologue to that global struggle against international fascism and aggression. Too late they have been brought to see that the Spanish Republicans were fighting the battle of all of us, and that the Franco forces were the agents of their German and Italian masters. Slowly they have come to understand that if they had listened to men like Quintanilla recent history might have been less terrible and fascist aggression cut down without recourse to world-wide war. There is bitterness in Quintanilla—the bitterness of the prophet who knew not only the heroism and the hope of the Republican Spain which our heedlessness helped to wreck, but the black ugliness of the corrupt reactionary Spain which we helped to survive. It is that black Spain—the Spain of decadent, diseased medievalism in thought and deed, a mockery of even the things it pretends to defend—which fills him with a loathing that gives every detail of his work such brutal power. Here is the Spain that Americans helped to make.

RICHARD WATTS, JR.

FRANCO'S BLACK SPAIN

1

Wherein General Franco dreams pleasantly among his valiant fellow crusaders, a peer among equals.

2

There was much irony in the Spanish prologue to the Second World War—such as the fact that the men who made Spain the subservient tool of Germany and Italy called themselves "Nationalists." Here the Caudillo—the Leader—appears to find nothing ironical in the way he, too, is being led. Anyway, General Franco must have found it less humiliating to be pulled through history with a ring in his nose by powerful Nazi Germany than to be pushed along by his other great ally, fatuous, incompetent Fascist Italy.

PNF

3

The Moor, too, found himself a crusader for Christian Civilization. Not the least striking instance of the Spanish Civil War's savage irony was that Franco's fascists—who proudly proclaimed that they were carrying on the chivalrous tradition of the Spanish knights who had driven the Moors from the sacred soil of their country, crying, "Death to the Moorish infidel!"—brought in Moorish troops by the thousands to fight their fellow countrymen.

4

The Moor, it is true, did have something to avenge. He certainly had no reason to cherish the Christian virtues of kindness and charity as practiced by the Spanish generals who ruled him in his own country. But it was not against these generals that the Moor directed his talents for killing and looting. It was against the Spanish people, who were not his enemies.

Luis Quintanilla

5

It was an outstanding victory of the Spanish generals that, in the widely proclaimed interest of saving their country from atheistic barbarism, they brought in the Moors, who were hardly civilized Christians, to indulge in frenzies of slaughter and burning and rape in a land that happened to be both civilized and Christian.

6

Street Scene, Franco Spain, circa 1938. One of the more peaceful episodes in the fight against Bolshevism—the Moorish defenders of Christian Civilization at the popular sport of quarreling over their loot.

7

Trade in Franco Spain. Despite the war, business was by no means at a standstill in Franco's city of Caceres in 1937. The Moorish crusaders were busy turning an honest peseta selling ears of slain atheist Bolsheviks to souvenir-hunting defenders of Christianity. (It was recalled at this time that when Franco was a mere captain of troops in Spanish Morocco in 1914, the Moors under his command were in the habit of parading with the heads of their enemies slung from their artillery.)

ARRIBA ESPAÑA
OREJAS
1 PTS

8

After Spanish civilization had been saved for Franco and Adolf Hitler, the Moorish crusaders departed—but they left memories behind them. It is a familiar enough matter in all wars, but it did seem particularly ironic as an aftermath to the Christian overthrow of the menace of Red Atheism.

9

Quite often, fascism seems to go hand in hand with sexual degeneracy. Black Spain has proved no exception to this rule.

10

What the Spanish Republicans saw when they retook the town of Peguerinos after the Moors had held it for just two hours. It was a small incident among so much horror, but it was so characteristic it could stand for thousands of other episodes.

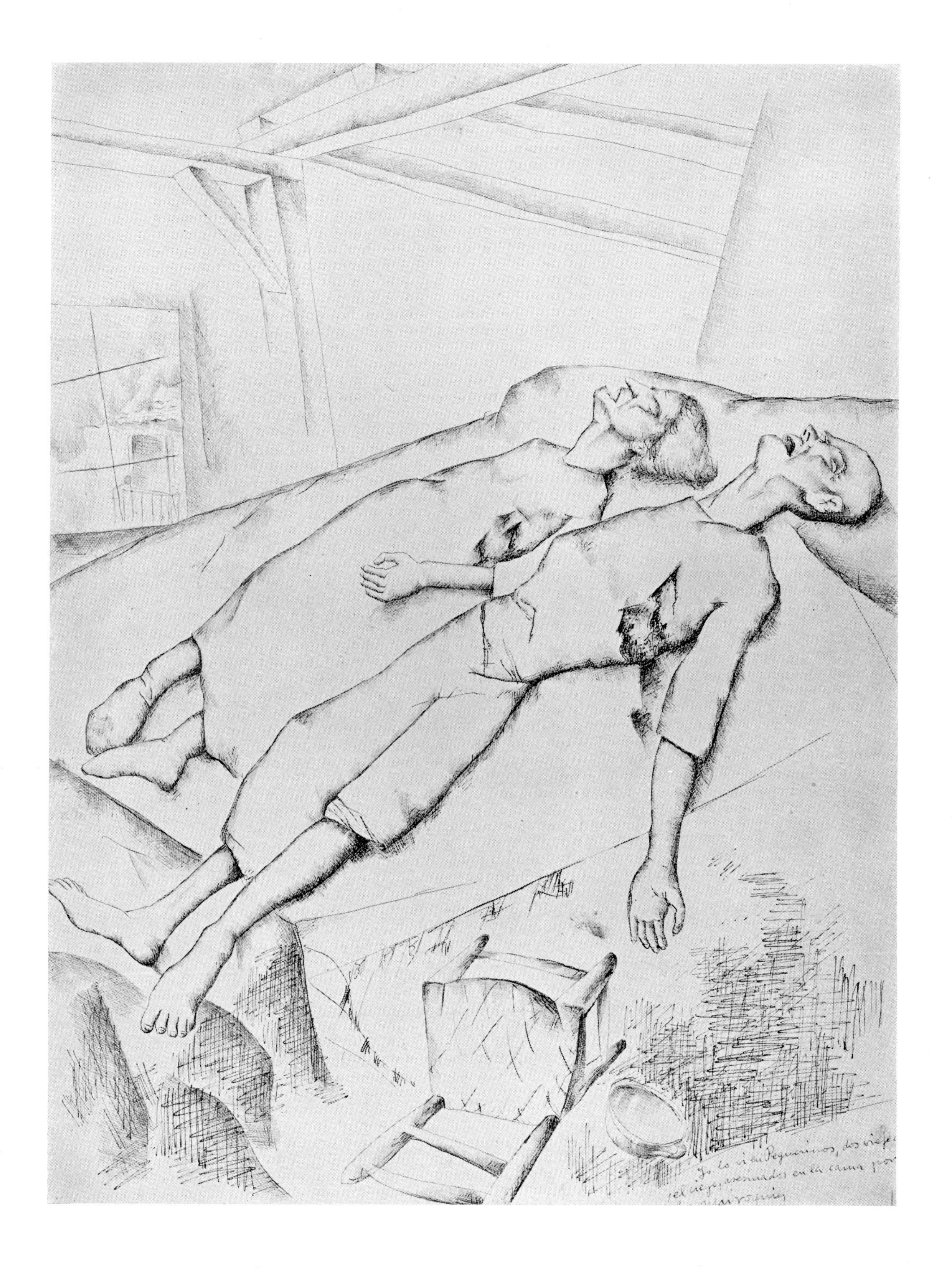
Yo lo vi en Pegueriños, dos viejos
y el ciego, asesinados en la cama por

11

The Civil Guard. There are no more characteristic defenders of the ideals of Black Spain than these grim, cold, ruthless ex-soldiers, with their black cloaks, their patent-leather hats, and their chill cruelty. Once a well-disciplined rural police, created to suppress banditry, they have become the most hated of all the official upholders of Franco's New Order. The worst thing about them in the eyes of Spanish patriots is that they are men of the people who have been trained to strike down their comrades, and do so with a kind of impersonal relish. These are characteristic types, realistically studied.

12

One of the jobs of the Civil Guard was to transfer from jail to jail some of the thousands of political prisoners that Franco's Holy War made of the once free men and women of the Spanish Republic. Quintanilla suggests that their frugal meal does nothing to soften the bored ferocity of the Guardsmen as they go about their appointed task.

13

The Civil Guard appeared to find particular relish in setting upon one of their victims when some of his family happened to be present.

Luis Quintanilla

14

The punishment called "the swing" was the Civil Guard's idea of a genuine lark.

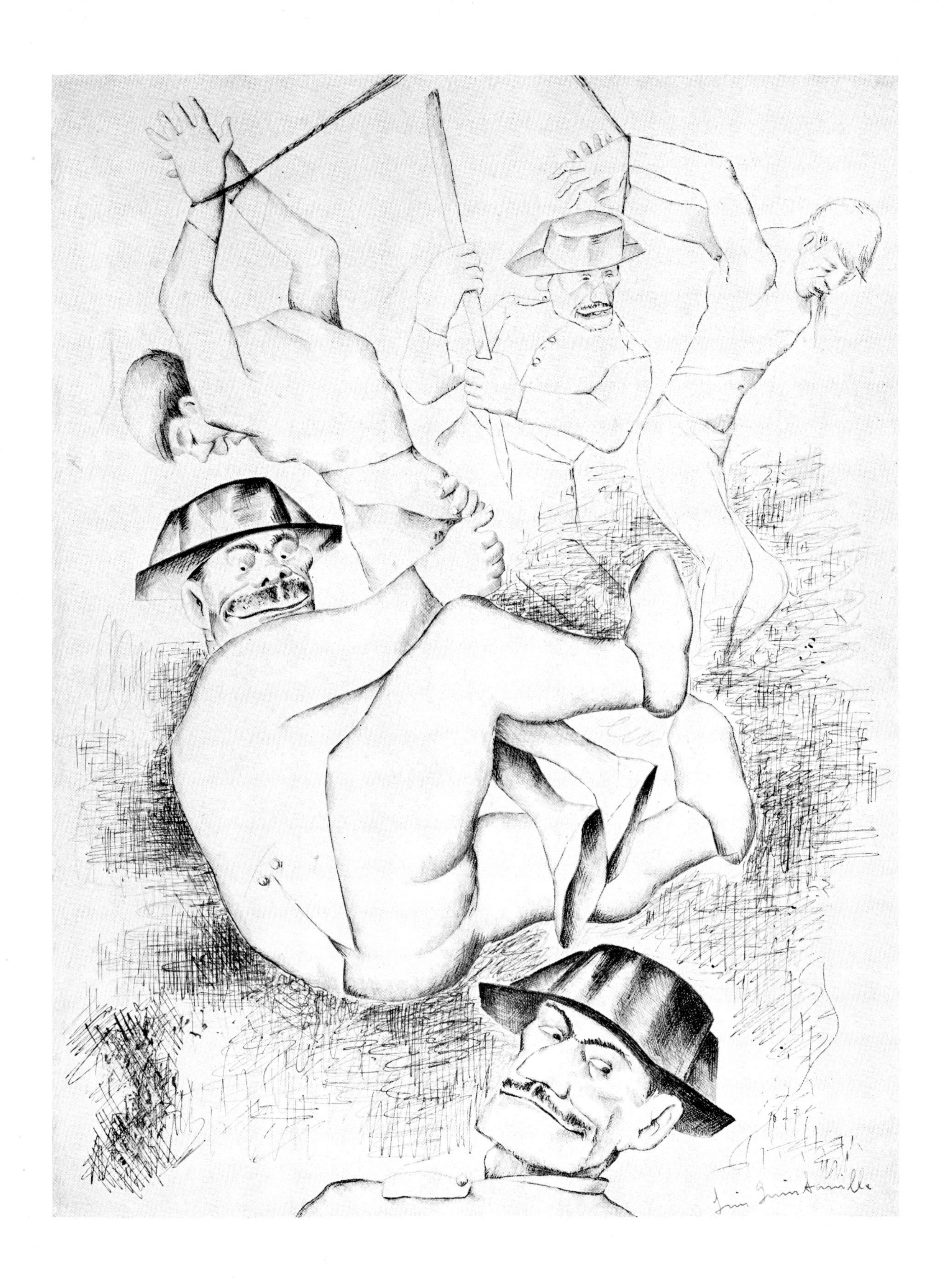

15

The treatment known as "the purge" was a lot of fun, too. The gentlemen of the Civil Guard are stolid fellows, rarely given to the luxury of relaxing their grim features, and the evidence is that only the sadistic pleasure of some casual torture inflicted on their Republican fellow countrymen permitted them the weakness of an occasional almost human smile.

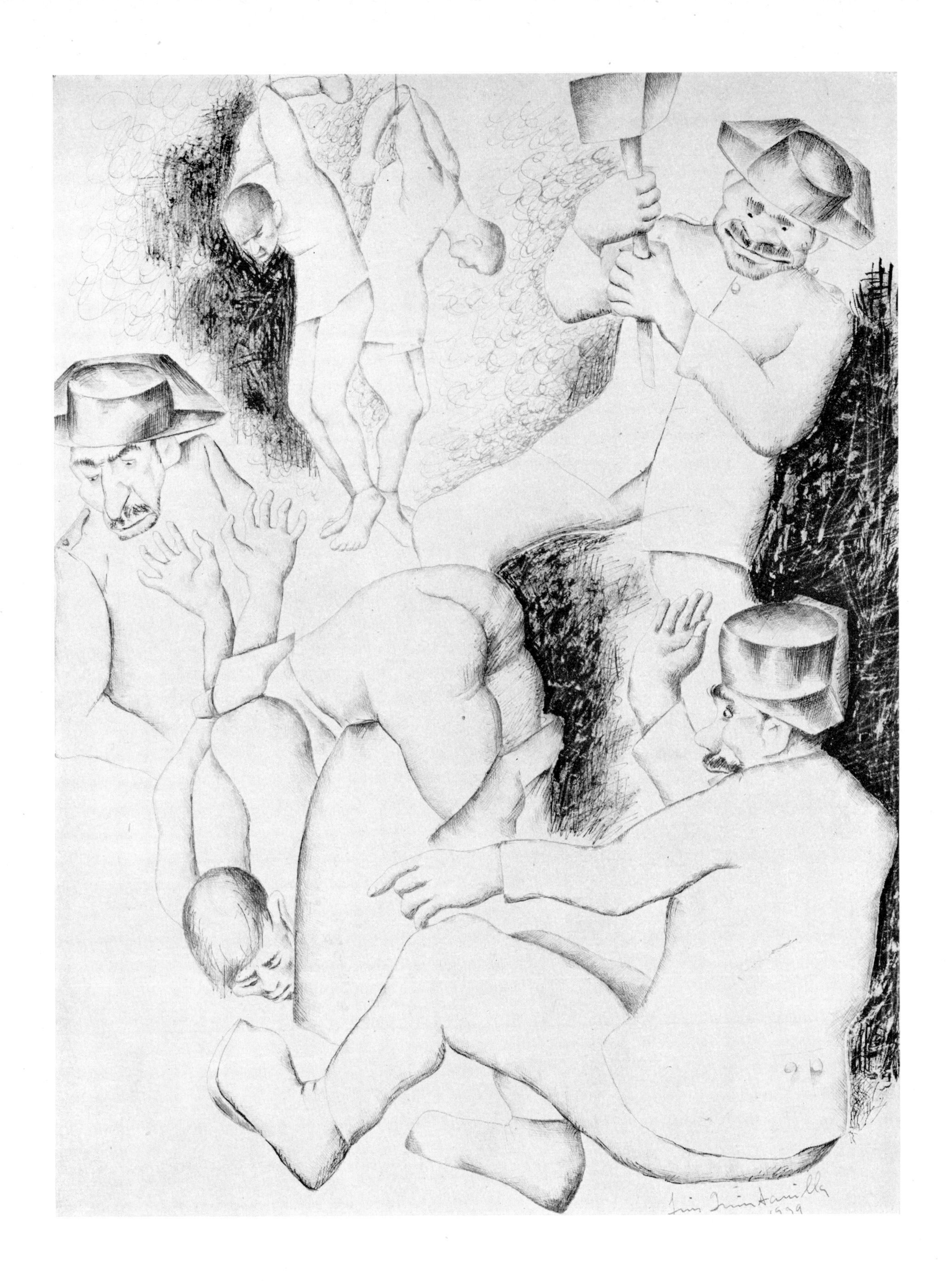

16

Then there was the sport to be had with women about to become mothers.

17

Out of the deepest pit of hypocrisy in Franco's Black Spain came the ignorance, savagery, and corruption that goes under the name of religion, but has in actuality seized upon a great and historic faith and turned it into a cruel parody of itself. Thousands of devout Catholics, knowing that their faith was not bound up with the social and political reaction which had proclaimed itself the Spanish manifestation of their religion, fought on the side of the Republic—particularly among the Basques, where priests battled side by side with laymen. It was their conviction to the death that the name and spirit of their Church had been perverted by a brutal and stupid oligarchy that kept the people in poverty and ignorance for its own material interest, while it hypocritically talked about a Christianity it never practiced or understood.

18

The man who apparently claims the distinction of giving to the world an expression that stands high in modern infamy. It is this General Mola, late leader of the fanatical soldiers from medieval Navarre, who is credited with telling his followers as they approached Madrid: "Four of our columns are attacking the capital and within it a fifth column is waiting to rise against the Republic when we give the word." It was more than a hint of the Quislings to come, and might conceivably have served as a valuable warning in the Second World War that was soon to succeed its doomed prologue. The men of Navarre, incidentally, have a certain distinction of their own. Even Black Spain looks upon them as reactionaries.

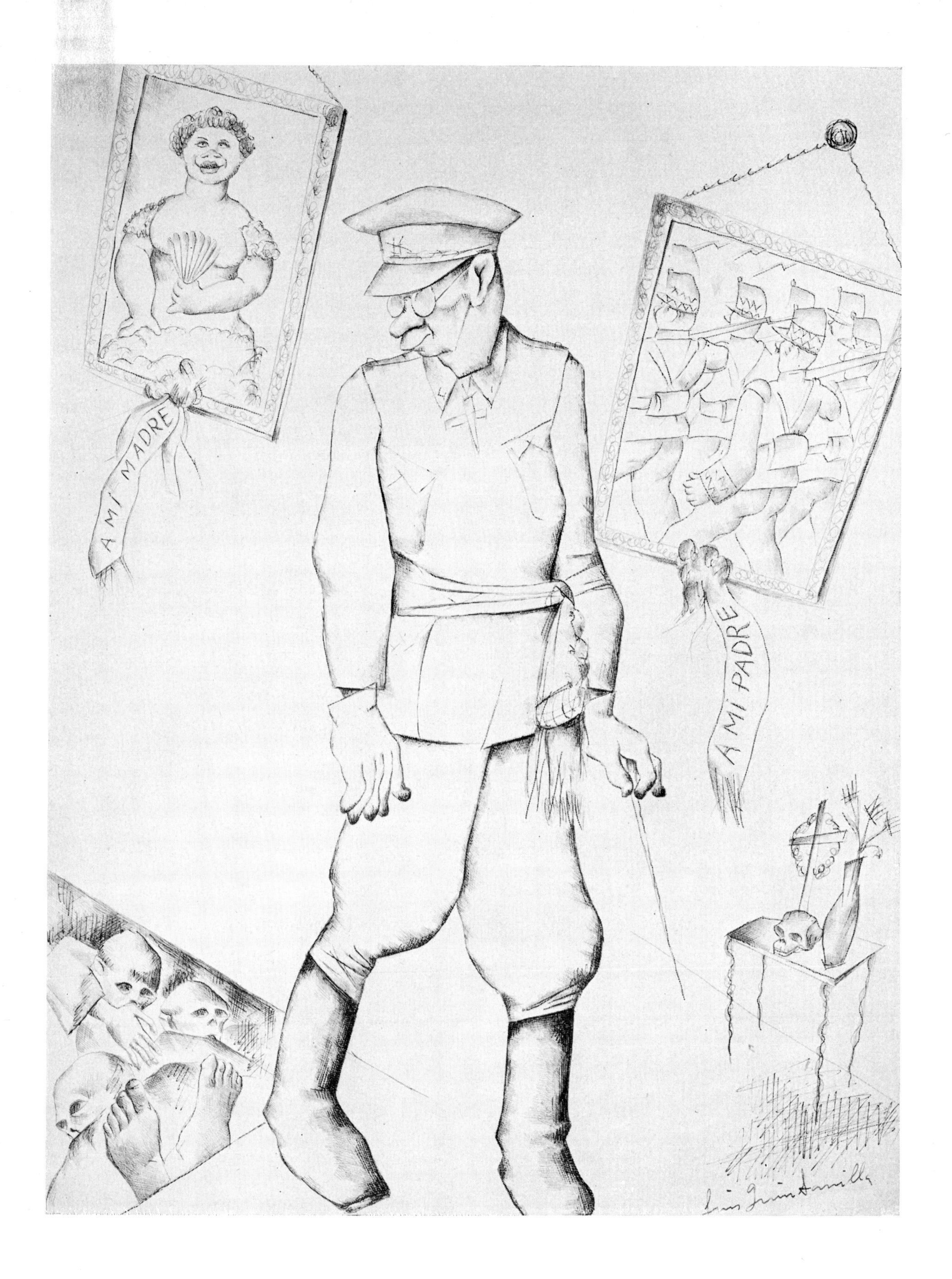
A MÍ MADRE
A MÍ PADRE

19

Even the gloomy Spanish fascists had their little joke. Under the Republic the peasants who had suffered from feudal rule appealed for agrarian reform and were given their own land to till. When Franco had his triumph these beneficiaries of the brief Republican rule were shot down in mass executions, while the fascists, with their rich sense of humor, said: "Here is real Agrarian Reform! A piece of land for every dead man."

Luis Quintanilla

20

Another jest highly regarded in Black Spain. Watching the condemned peasants dig their own graves prior to the mass executions.

Luis Quintanilla

21

There seems to have been a particular pleasure in executing schoolteachers. At least, it has been estimated that nearly eleven thousand of them were shot down by Franco's Crusaders for the crime of telling young Spaniards about such things as liberty and equality. Of course, their books were burned, too.

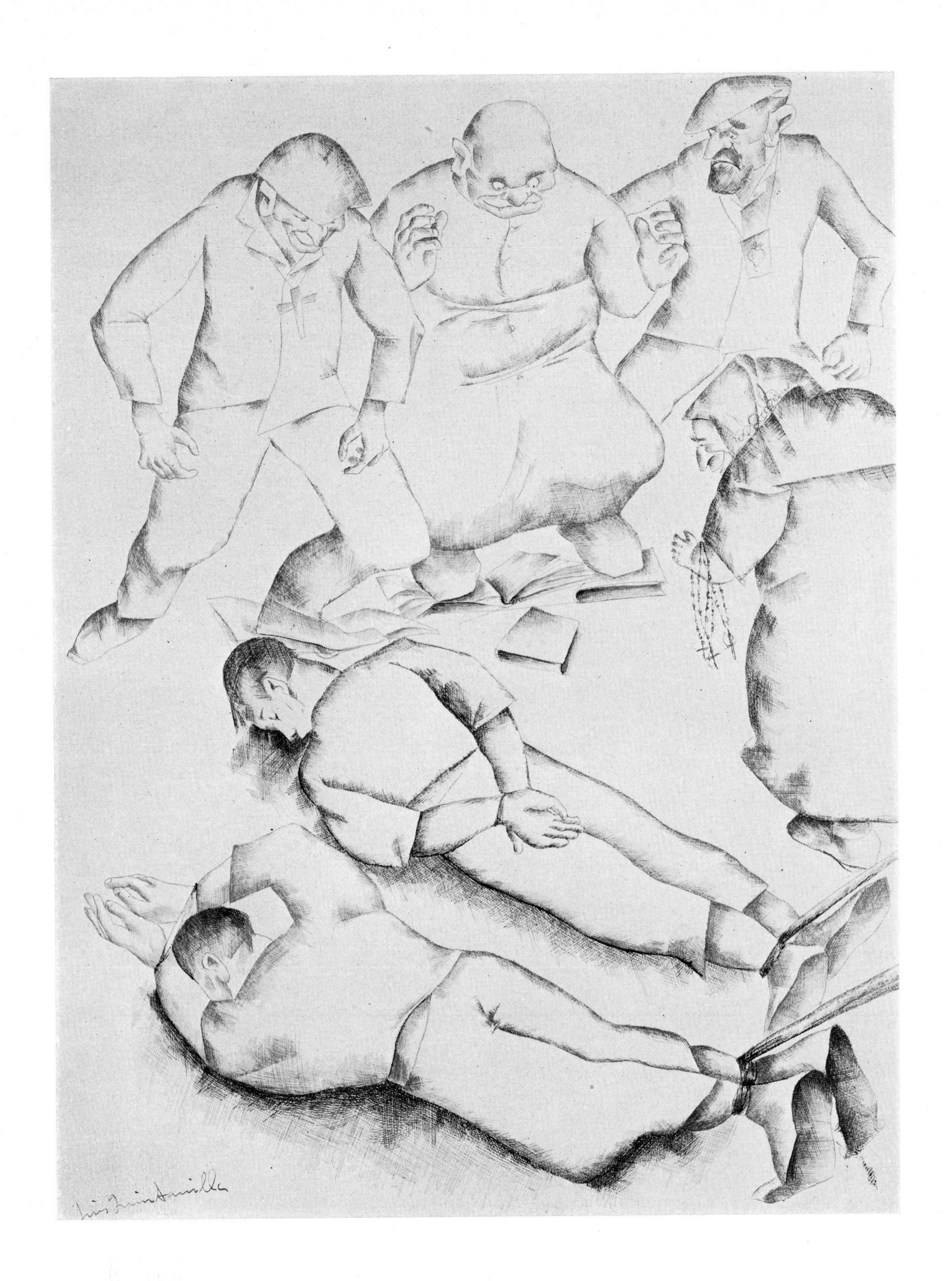

22

The fanatic among fanatics: the Requete from Navarre, an anachronism from the Age of the Inquisition set down in Franco's Spain. A grim, brave fighter, and one so steeped in the spirit of medievalism that he looked upon his fascist allies as little better than Red Radicals.

23

The practice of looting by means of classifying a family as "Red," and therefore the proper prey of any defender of Christian Civilization, never failed to coincide with the best ideals of the Franco Crusade.

24

The Spanish people knew the pseudo-religious sadists who came up from the lowest depths of the urban slums to spread their destruction in the name of Heaven as "cavern-dwellers." The wives and daughters of Republican workers were among the favorite victims of the cavern-dwellers.

25

One of the great triumphs of the Franco Crusade was that it brought back to Spain those charming representatives of the decadent old aristocracy who had gracefully sat out the Republic in the cafés and on the fashionable beaches of France and Portugal. A little petulant because their Bourbon king was not restored with them, they managed to keep down their disappointment long enough to give Black Spain the honor of their presence.

26

The men of the master race who, with some slight aid from the sleeping democracies of the United States, Great Britain, and France, destroyed the Spanish Republic. When the first soldiers of the Reichswehr arrived in the Franco-controlled sections of Spain, they intended to land secretly, since it seemed to them impossible that the democracies would not object to this flagrant intervention against the legally established Spanish Republic. But that was the day of appeasement, and the United States, Britain, and France were so gullible—when they were not frankly hostile toward the struggling Republic—that the Nazis could throw off the mask, send some sixty thousand troops into Spain (at least that was the figure that once appeared in Goering's newspaper), and try out at leisure their methods of military terror. It was this blindness of the democracies toward Spain which more than anything else convinced Hitler that they would back down before any aggression and thus played a chief part in bringing about the Second World War.

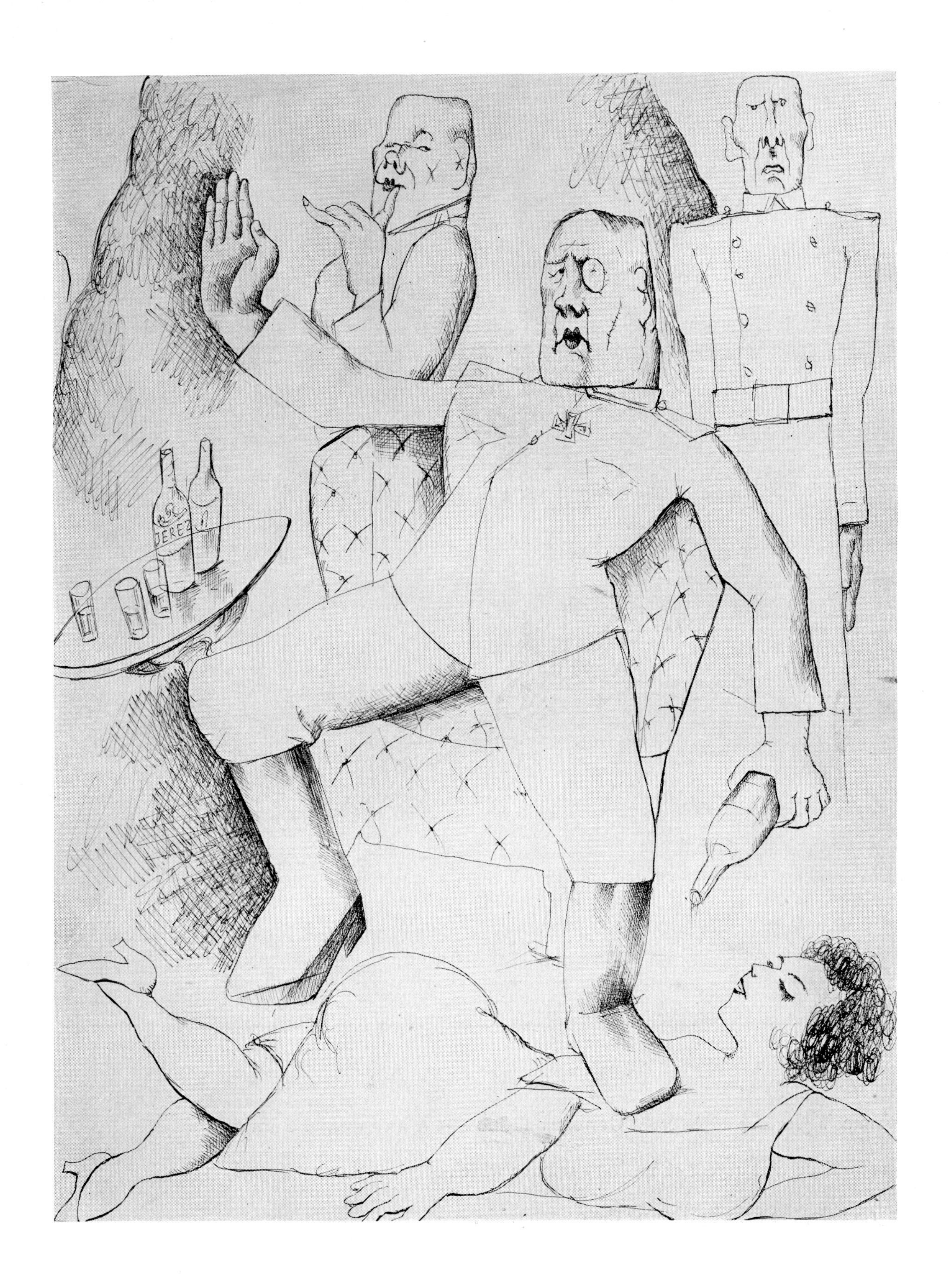
JEREZ

27

Franco's glorious allies from Germany found Spain a congenial training ground for that aspect of military science which they found particularly agreeable, the art of pillaging the countryside.

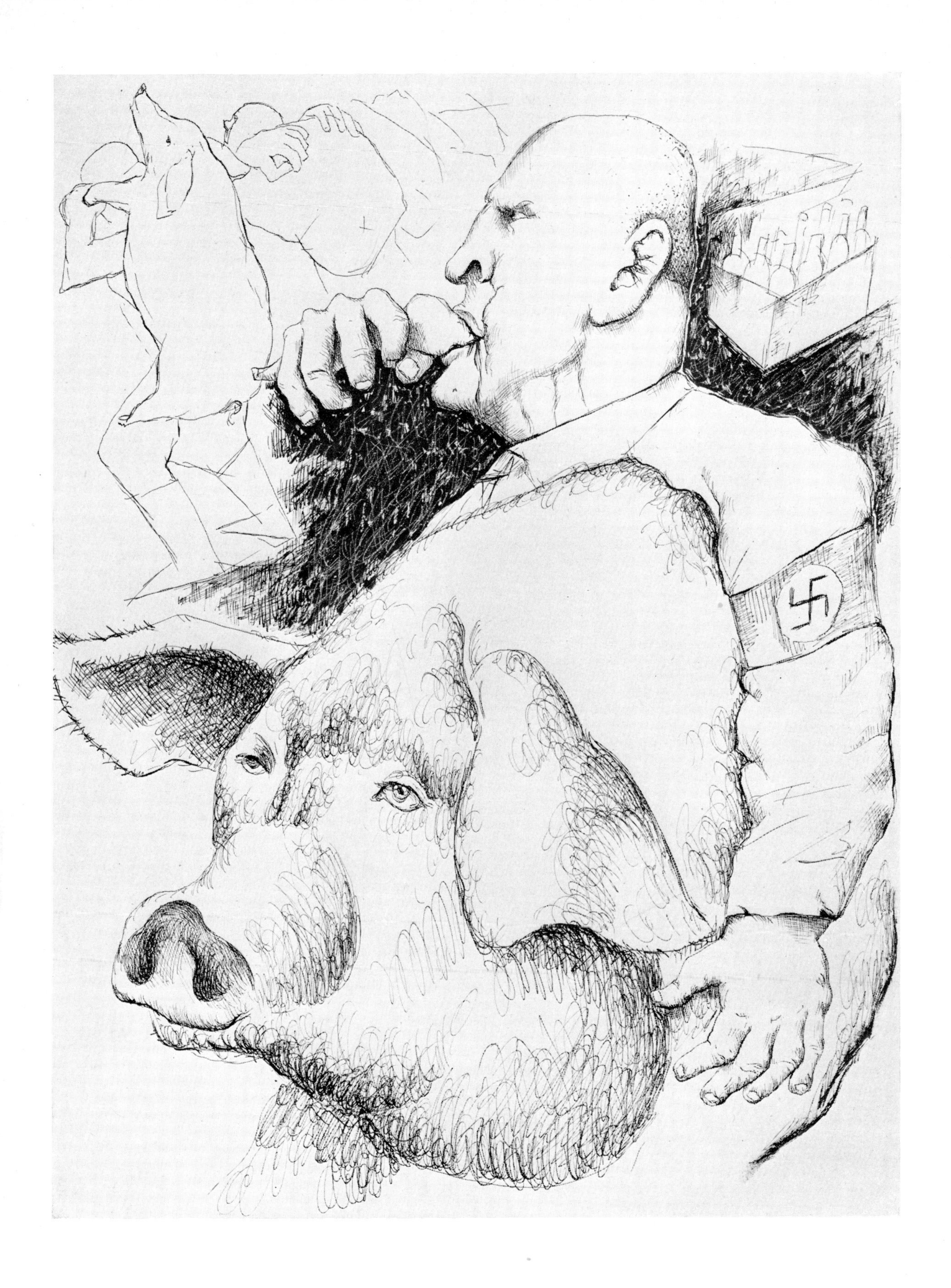

28

Nazi total warfare, as later demonstrated by Goering's air force on London, Coventry, and Rotterdam, found Republican Spain an ideal testing ground. Since the cities destroyed were "Red" cities and the civilians killed were "Red" civilians, the strong Christian protests that were forthcoming when the Republic protected itself against purely political clericalism were never heard.

29

Even the concentration camp, which the Nazis were later to make of all Europe, was tried out by the Germans in Spain.

30

The Nazi scientist established his laboratory in Franco Spain. It seemed to the Caudillo's German masters that the men and women of the land of their Spanish ally were ideal guinea pigs for those experiments in wholesale destruction and death that were later to turn the Nazi concentration camps into the charnel houses of Europe.

31

The Italian Fascist troops that were poured into Franco Spain by the thousands supplied a wry kind of comic relief to the Spanish tragedy. At least it is to their everlasting credit that they had no heart for Mussolini's burlesque imperialism. Their fellow countrymen who died in the Loyalist International Brigade proved that Italians know how to make war when they have something to fight about.

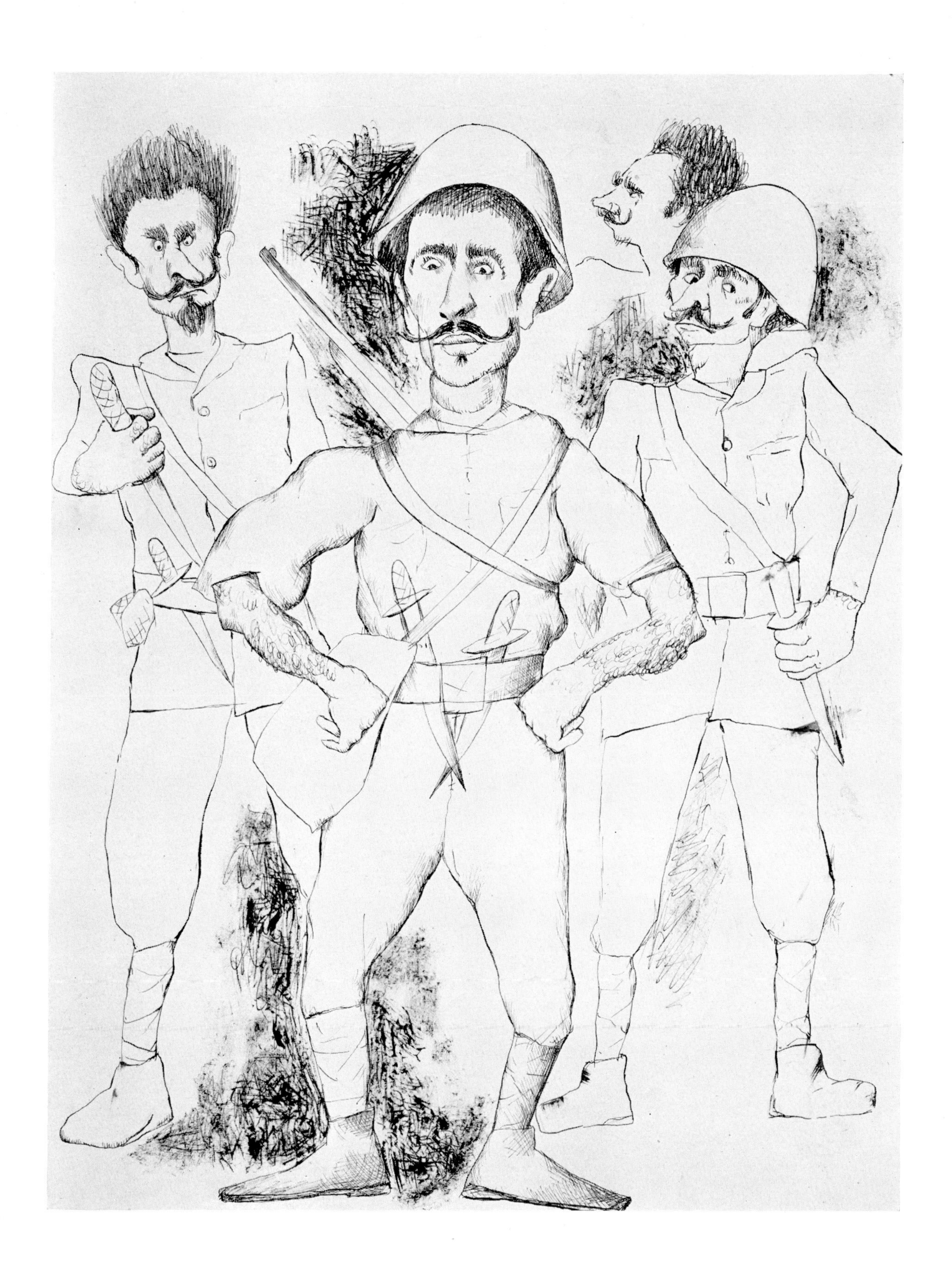

32

A characteristic pair of Mussolini's crusaders in Spain; obviously and sensibly an operatic aria or some good food was of more interest to them than military grandeur. It would have been difficult to find more unwilling "volunteers."

33

Mussolini's Roman heroes, as the soldiers of the Spanish Republic almost invariably saw them.

34

One of the most incredible characters in Black Spain was General Queipo de Llano, the drunken, blasphemous shouter of insults over his own radio station in Seville. "The Barbarian of Seville," as he was amiably called, finally became too violent for even his fascist friends and was quietly squelched.

35

The young Falange gangsters, who had been organized by Jose Primo de Rivera, son of the onetime dictator, numbered less than three thousand at the time Franco and his fellow militarists revolted against the Republic in July, 1936. Although they attempted a sort of philosophical rationale of fascism, they were clearly more interested in brawling and in picturesque uniforms.

36

The Falange grew in numbers as the revolt, thanks to its foreign backing and the fact that the Western democracies would not permit the Republic to arm itself, grew in strength. But the quality remained about the same.

37

Slowly the Spanish Republic was strangled and the land became a vast concentration camp, with the most disreputable jailers known to modern history.

38

The chivalry of the Spanish Falange was in the best tradition of the Franco Crusade.

39

The Falange triumphant in a Spain freed of decadent democracy.

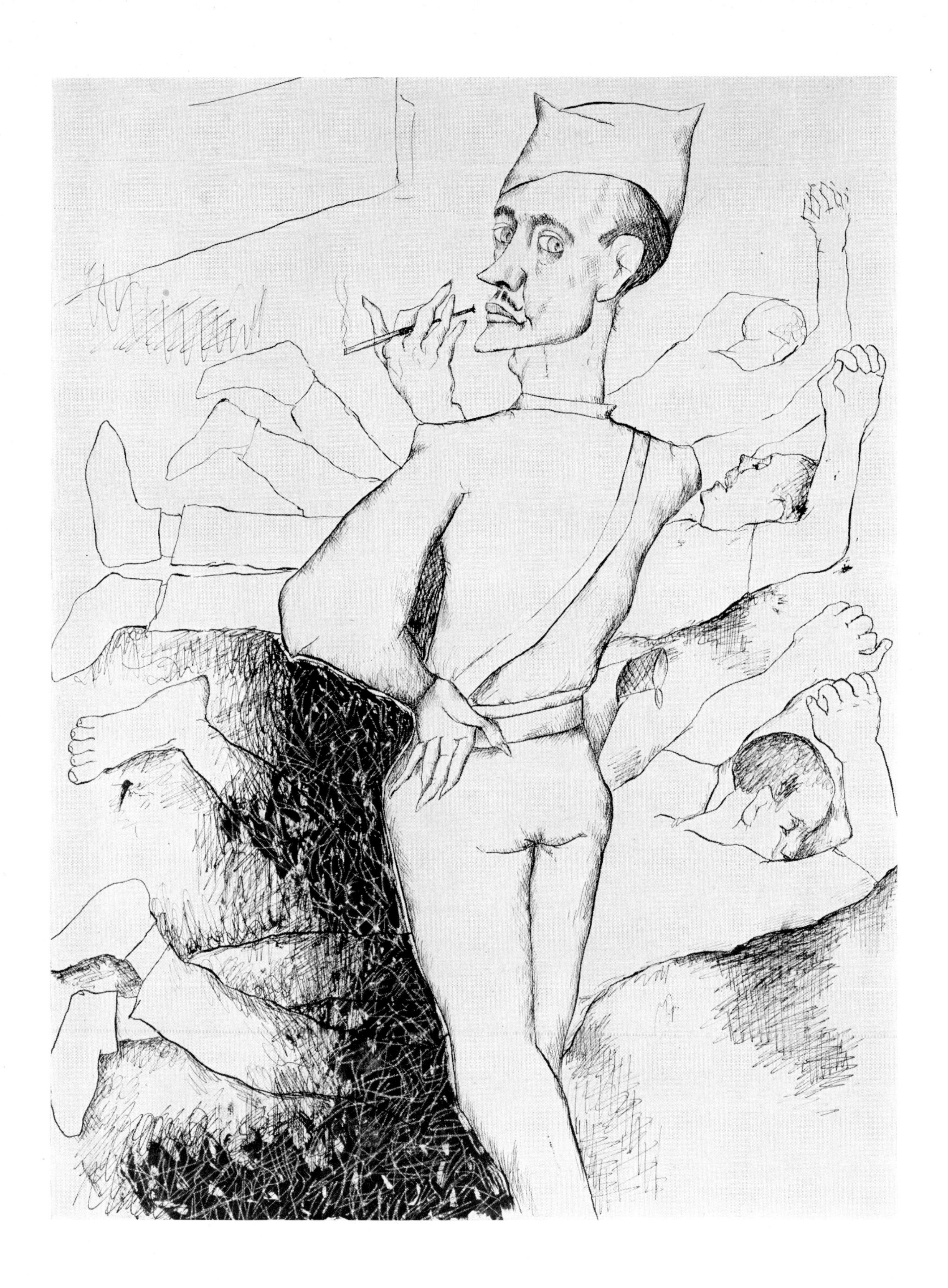

40

What was left was a nation in chains, crushed in body and spirit, sunk in poverty and desperation, dominated by a combination of bleak medievalism and modern totalitarianism, the flower of its people dead, imprisoned, or exiled—this is the Black Spain that our blindness helped to create.